The Backwoods Guide to

COMPUTER LINGO

Published by Cowsamungus Publishing
1 Scale Avenue
Unit 53
Rutland, Vermont 05701

Printed in U.S.A.

First edition 1995.
Second edition 1995.

ISBN 0-9649972-1-5

The Backwoods Guide to

COMPUTER LINGO

written by Dave Nilsen • illustrated by Chris Mathewson

MODEM - What you did to the hay fields.

DOT MATRIX -
Farmer Matrix's
old lady.

PRINTER - Someone who can't write in cursive.

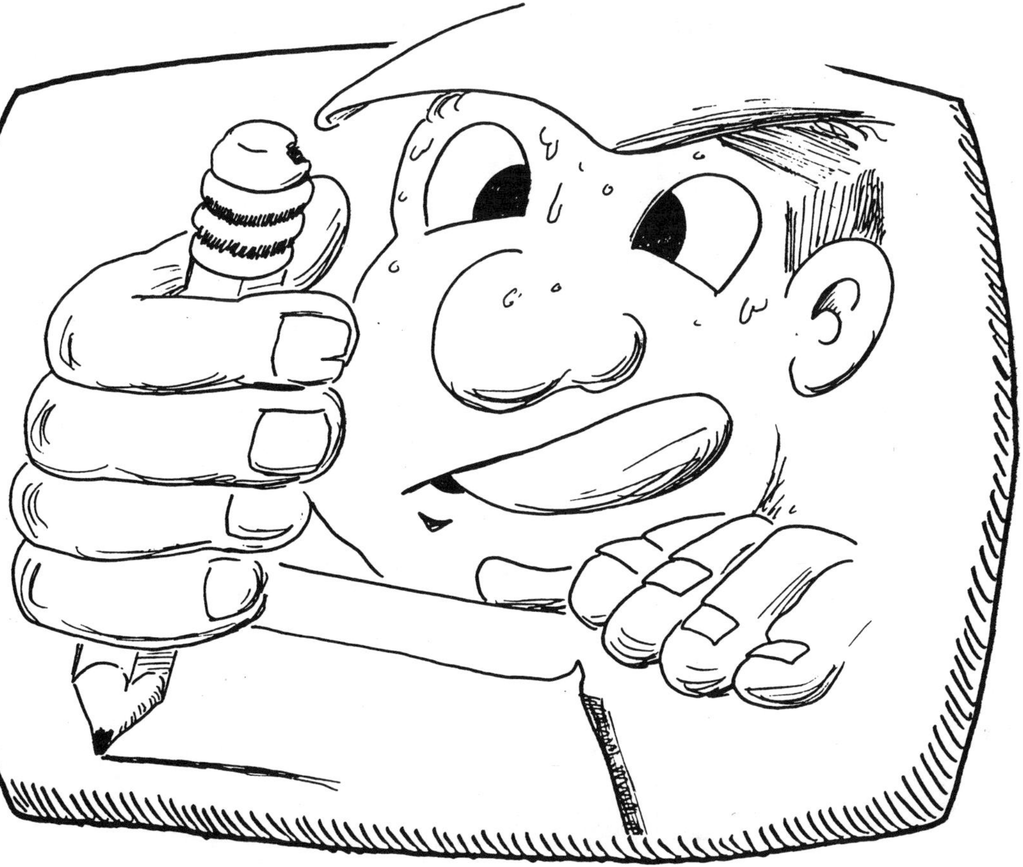

LAP TOP -
Where little kids
feel comfy.

KEYBOARD - Where you hang yer keys.

TRUK
CAR

ELECTRONIC MAIL - Bathroom readin' material.

RADIO MART-WINTER 1983
TV'S
VCR'S

LOG ON - Makin' the wood stove hotter.

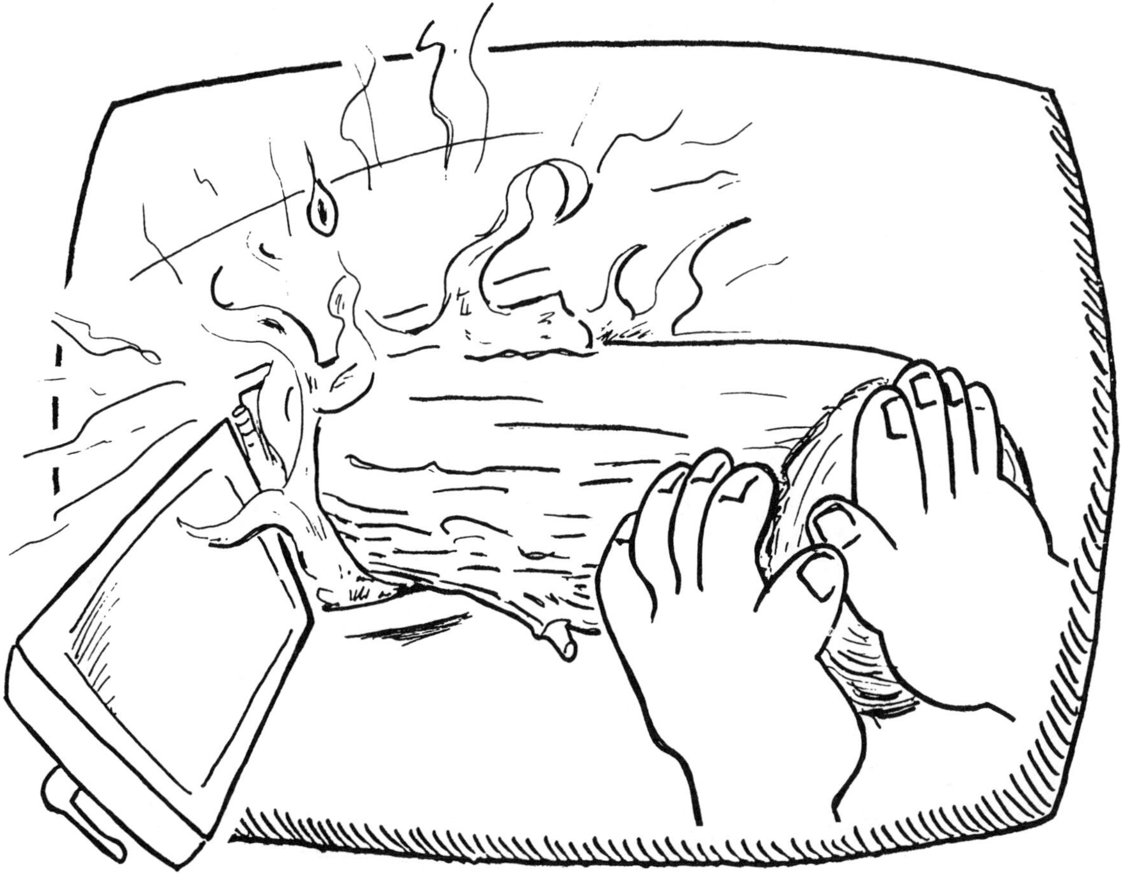

LOG OFF -
Don't add wood.

MONITOR - Keep an eye on the woodstove.

DOWNLOAD - Gettin' the firewood off the pick-up.

MEGA HERTZ-
When yer
not careful
downloadin'.

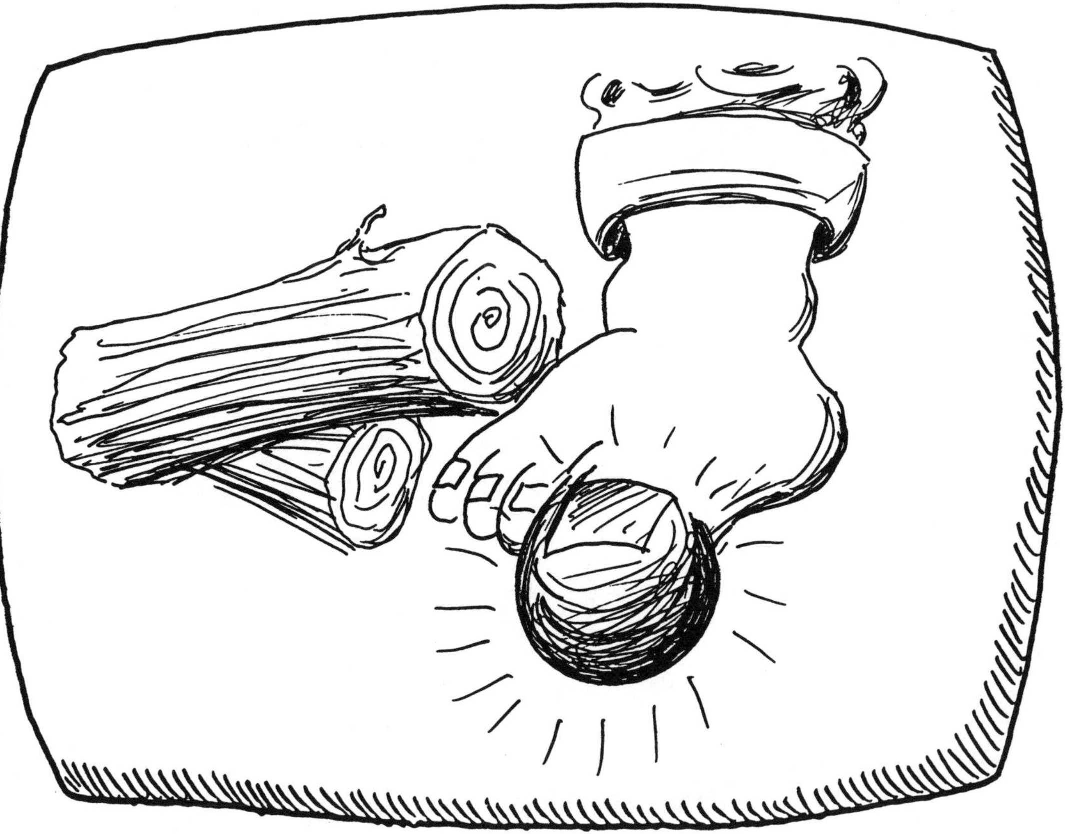

FLOPPY DISC - What you get from pilin' too much firewood.

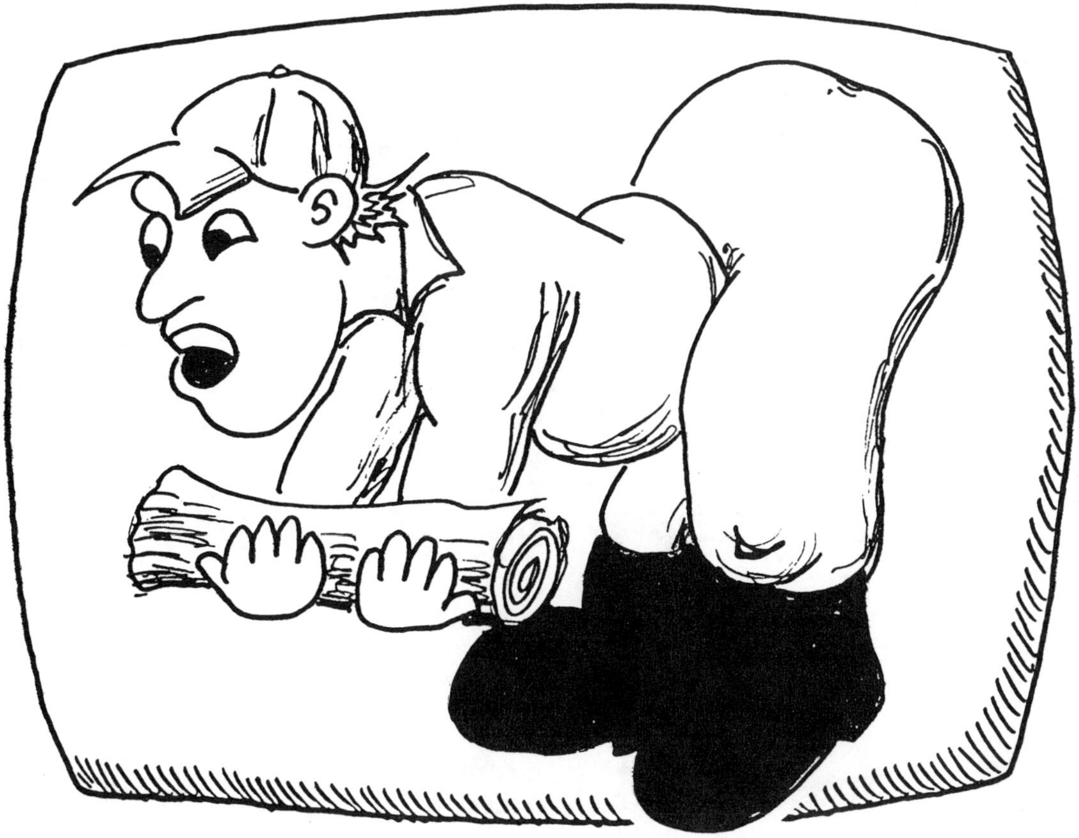

DOS (Disc Operating System) - The equipment the Doc uses when you have a floppy disc.

RAM - The hydraulic thingy that makes the woodsplitter work.

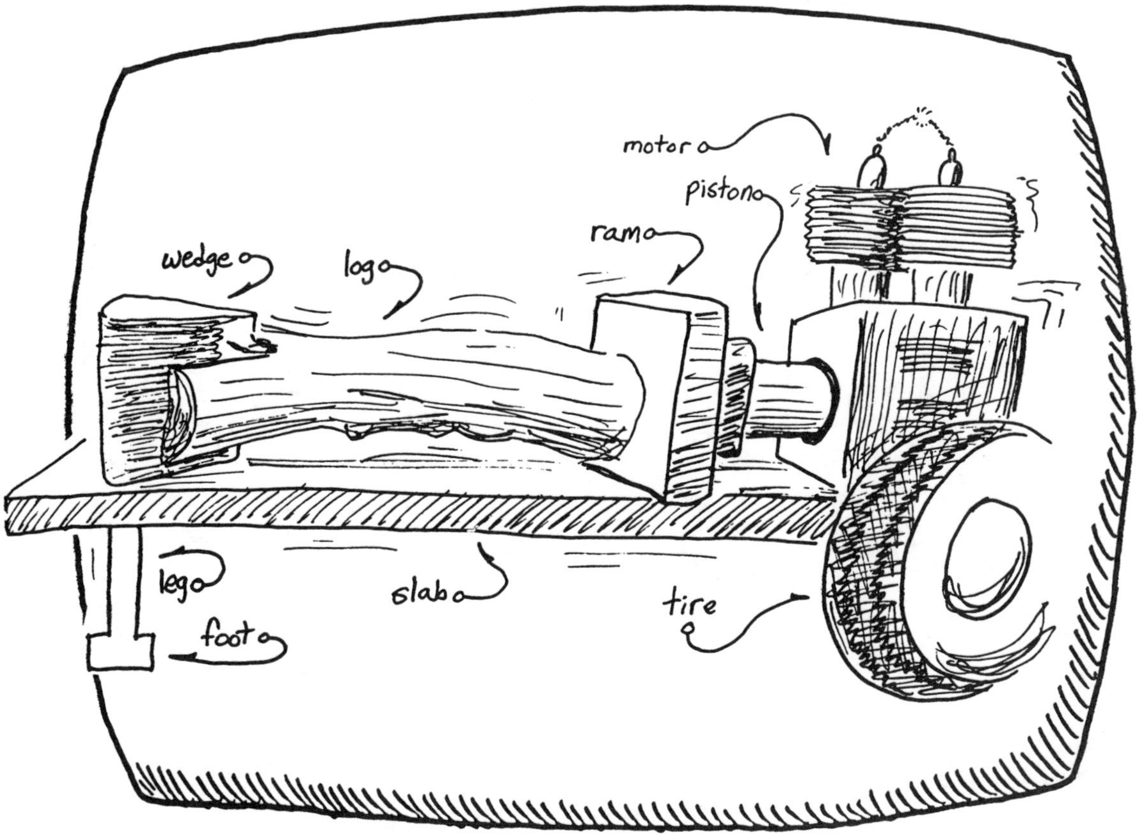
motoro
pistono
ramo
wedgeo
logo
lego
slabo
tire
footo

HARDWARE -
What you fix the
wood splitter with.

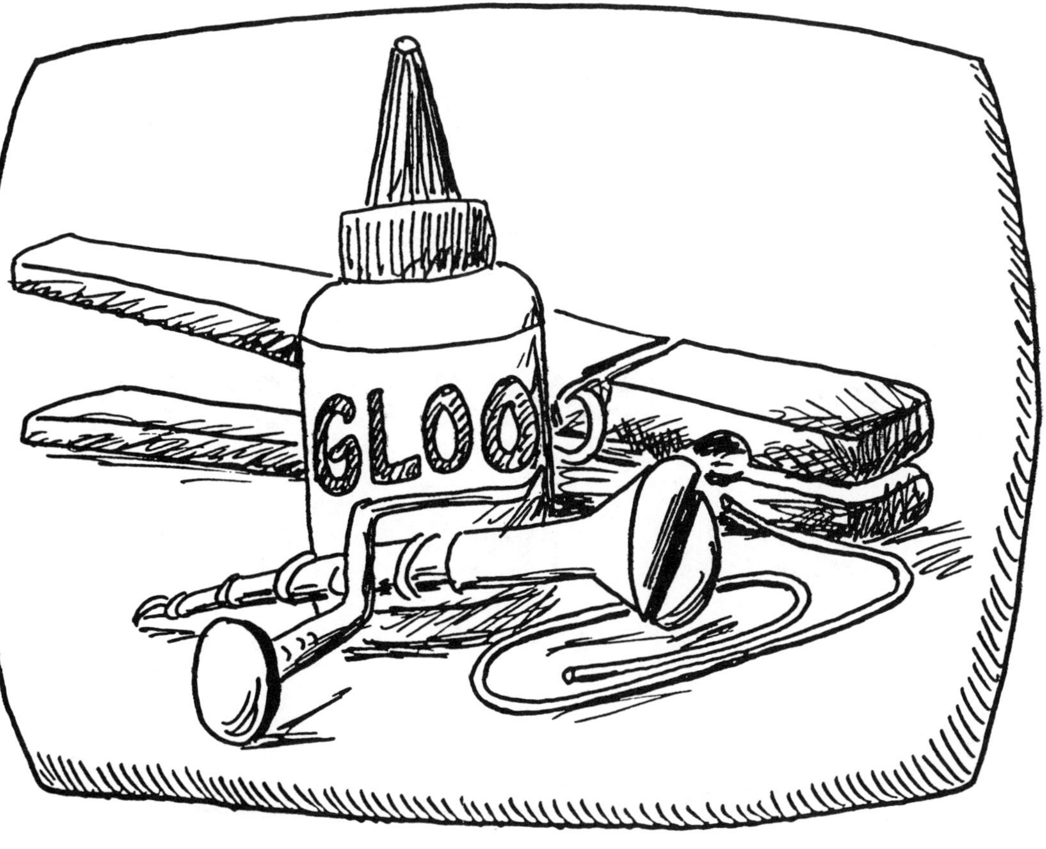
GLOO

SOFTWARE -
Them there plastic
eatin' utensils.

HARD DRIVE -
Gettin' home in
mud season.

PROMPT -
What you wish the mail was in mud season.

486 MB - One of them fancy imported cars.

MOUSE - What eats the horses grain in the barn.

MAIN FRAME - The part of the barn that holds the roof up.

WINDOWS - What to shut when it's 20 below.

SCREEN - What you need for black fly season.

BYTE - What black flies do.

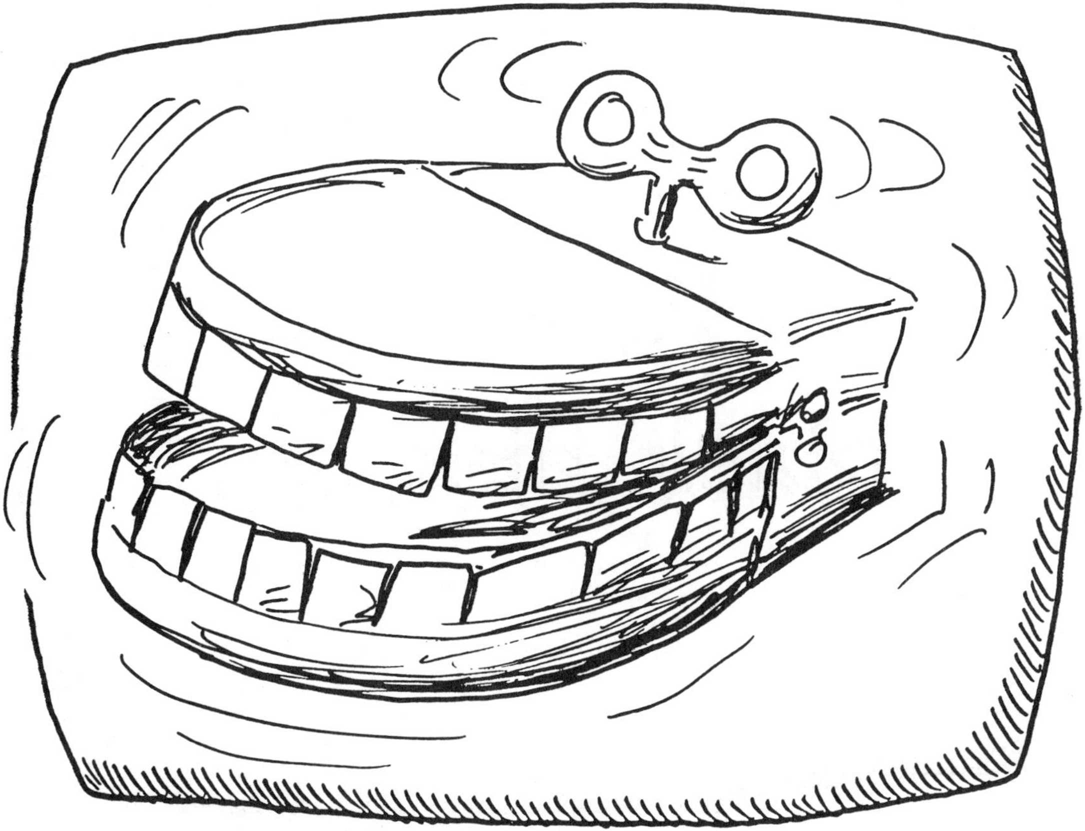

PORT -
Fancy wine.

LE EXPENSIF
PORT
PRODUIT D'FR

ENTER -

C'mon in!

RANDOM ACCESS MEMORY - You can't remember how much that new rifle cost when your wife asks.

GUN SHOP
$

DIGITAL - Like your alarm clock.

1037

APPLE - If you don't know, I ain't tellin'.

PROGRAM - What's on TV when there's reception.

FAX - Dunno... Ma would never talk to us about it.

CD ROM - The foreigner at the bank that sells retirement accounts.

TELLER
$$$
BUY!
OWN!
HELLO
Rom

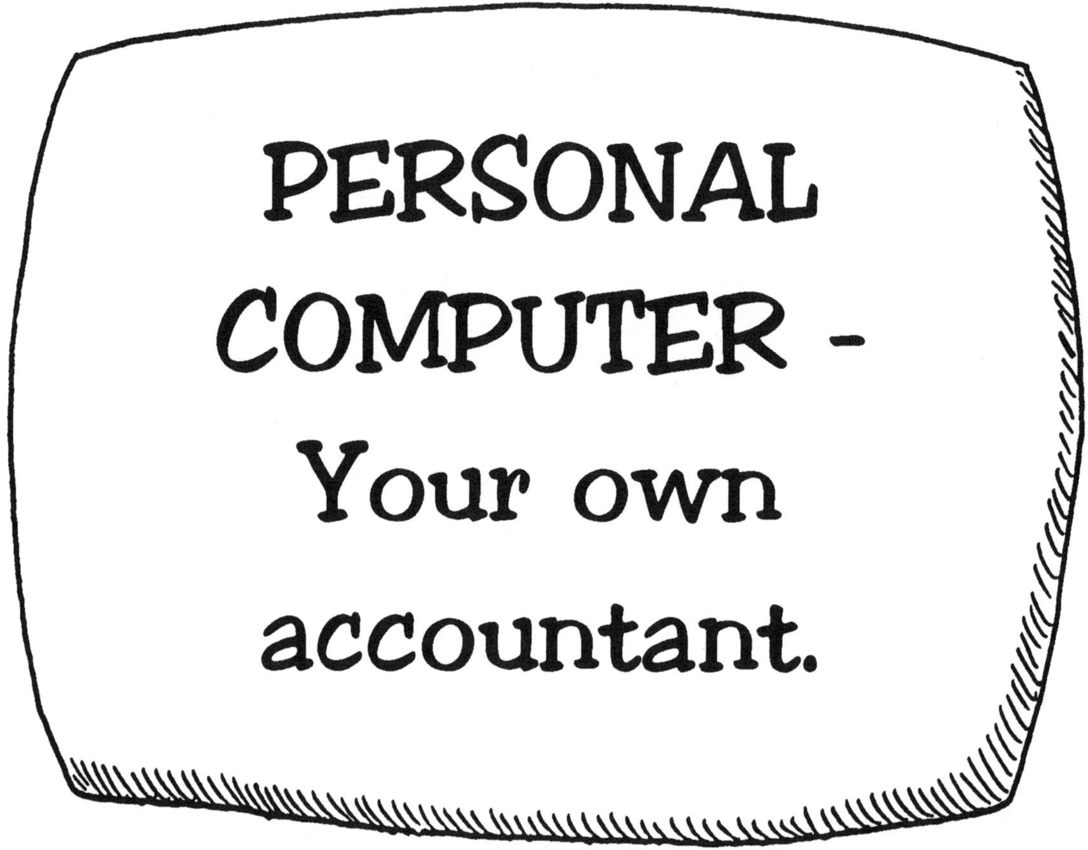
PERSONAL
COMPUTER -
Your own
accountant.

3.17

DIN - The noise at the barn dance.

SERIAL - What's for breakfast.

CHIP - What to munch on.

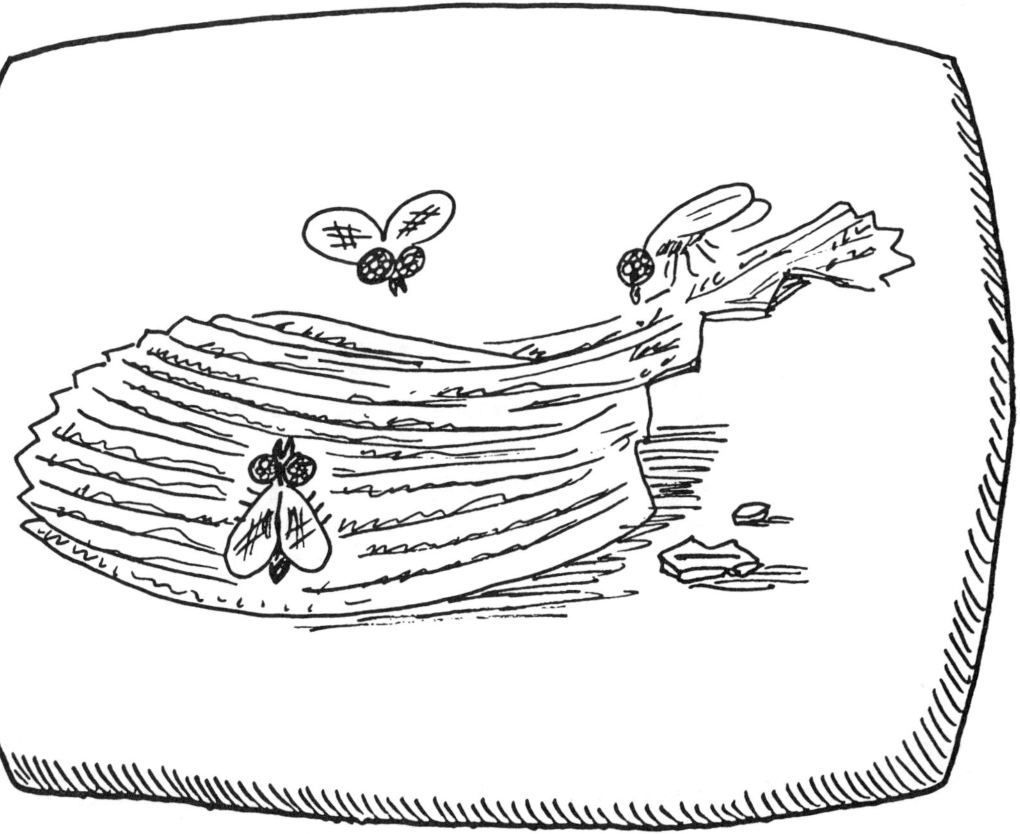

LASER - Someone less ambitious than you.

Fred's

INFRARED -
Where the
left-overs go.

FRED'S
PLUMBING &
HEATING